TALL SHIPS

THE MAGIC OF SAIL

DEAN SERVER

NEW LINE BOOKS

Fax: (888) 719-7723

E-mail: info@newlinebooks.com

Printed and bound in China

ISBN 978-1-59764-145-6

Visit us on the web!

www.newlinebooks.com

Author: Dean Server

Publisher: Robert M. Tod
Senior Editor: Edward Douglas
Associate Editor: Amy Handy
Picture Researcher: Robin Raffer
Book Designer: Mark Weinberg
Typesetting: Command-O Design

CONTENTS

INTRODUCTION

Tall sailing ships dominated the world's major oceans for centuries while fulfilling many important functions. They carried millions of tons of cargo, provided transportation for millions of passengers, and fought in every war. But there was much more than just a practical side to the great ships. With their grand and majestic appearance, they were also awesome pieces of art, capable of creating great excitement.

In the nineteenth century, it was common for huge crowds to come out just to get a glimpse of the newest tall ship. In 1853, when the gigantic Great Republic was launched in Boston Harbor, the interest in her appearance was so vast that a crowd of more than fifty thousand appeared, even though transportation to the location was quite difficult and primitive at the time. The Great Republic was so big it would fill any stadium in the world today. The newly launched ship stretched more than 325 feet (100 meters) in length, with sails reaching heights of more than 200 feet (60 meters). The huge gathering jammed every available spot along the harbor to view the great ship.

In the parlance of the sea, a "tall" ship specifically has at least three masts, all with what are called "square" sails (which are actually more rectangular). That type of sail can be strung higher because it is laid across the mast. The extra height of the sails on tall ships allows them to utilize the wind better and to sail faster. Other large vessels—specifically the bark and the barkentine—also have three masts, but they include sails that are not square.

Many of today's sailing ships were built to resemble the great ships of previous centuries. But they do not perform the same services that sailing ships did in the past; they are not a major source of transportation, they no longer carry cargo, and they have not fought in wars since early in the nineteenth century. Yet even with little remaining practical use, tall ships remain popular. Even amid the marvels of the modern world, the descendants of the great sailing ships of the past are still quite capable of attracting huge audiences with their imposing physical presence.

In 1976 more than six million people lined the nearest coasts to watch an array of tall ships sail past New York City in honor of the bicentennial celebration in the United States. More than 220 sailing ships from 31 countries participated in those festivities, which took more than five years to coordinate. A crowd of nearly two million gathered again in New York in 1986 as 200 more sailing ships paid

RIGHT: **Like most such gatherings, the 1992 assembling of tall ships in Boston attracted large crowds, including this one on Black Falcon Pier.**

4

TALL SHIPS

homage to the Statue of Liberty's centennial. And another fleet of more than 200 ships sailed into Sydney Harbor in January 1988 to take part in Australia's bicentennial. More than two million people watched as eleven tall ships that had sailed to Sydney from England reenacted the original ship landings from the eighteenth century.

The tall sailing ships that dominated the world's oceans by the eighteenth century and remain popular today are the culmination of nearly five thousand years of sailing development. Egyptian sailors first learned how to hoist sails to use the wind in about 3000 B.C. Other nations ruled the seas for long periods, including the Greeks and the Romans. The Viking ships of Scandinavia dominated the waters for almost four centuries. Later, the Venetians had the best-equipped fleet and controlled much of the Mediterranean commerce. Through the centuries, ships became larger and more efficient, while sails became more effective.

The many centuries of progress finally produced the most glorious sailing ships of them all, the clipper ships of the mid-nineteenth century. With their long length, lean hulls, and high sails, they were able to carry large cargo over the world's major oceans while generating much more speed than earlier ships. The clippers could travel as much as two hundred miles (350 kilometers) more per day than the heavier sailing ships of previous years. Originally they were known as Yankee clippers, because the earliest ones were all built in North America, mostly in New England in the 1840s and 1850s. But in subsequent years, as the North American market for such ships declined, many large and important clippers were built in England. The tea merchants in Britain offered special bonuses to the ships that returned to England the quickest with their Chinese tea. This created a clipper-building frenzy in that country that lasted through the 1860s.

While many centuries of advancements eventually produced the magnificent tall ships of the nineteenth century, progress also led to their gradual disappearance from the seas. Although Robert Fulton's First steamship met success in 1807, sailing ships continued to dominate the oceans with their superior speed for several more decades. But late in the century, ship designers and engineers had figured out how to build steamships efficient enough at sea to match the speeds of the fastest clippers. A few years later, the steamships were traveling much faster. The coal that provided fuel for the steam engines and had been hard to obtain in many locations through most of the nineteenth century became much more readily available. And shortcuts enabled by the creations of the Suez and Panama Canals allowed steamships to travel much shorter distances that required less fuel. The tall ships were either too big to go through the narrow openings of the new canals, or could not generate enough speed to get through sections of still air.

Those sailing ships that remained in service in the twentieth century were soon replaced and have all but disappeared from the world's oceans, at least in their traditional military and commercial roles. But the ones remaining, and the legends of those of the past, will continue to inspire new generations with their grace, beauty, and power.

OPPOSITE: **Viking ships dominated the seas for several centuries. As seen in this painting of American, James G. Tyler, the Viking ships sported one large triangular sail, with a sharp bow featuring ferocious-looking ornamentation.**
FOLLOWING PAGE: **Massachusetts was the location for the construction of the great Yankee clipper ships of the mid-nineteenth century. Robert Salmon captured a typical view of those days in his portrayal of Boston harbor.**

THE EVOLUTION

ONE

OF THE TALL SHIP

The Egyptians were apparently both the first to utilize sails at sea and also the first to construct a ship by fitting together planks of wood. This made their boats large and sturdy with a solid foundation, replacing the previous method of tying reeds together. The original large Egyptian vessels, which journeyed on the Nile powered by only one large rectangular sail, stretched to lengths of more than 200 feet (61 meters) and carried as much as 750 tons (680 metric tons) of cargo. The primitive yet sturdy ancient ships did not generate much speed. The Egyptian vessels only traveled about 5 miles (8 kilometers) an hour.

The History of Sailing

Since those ancient times, ships have continually gotten bigger, stronger, and faster. By 500 B.C., Greece was the dominant power of the Mediterranean region, and their shipbuilders made several significant contributions to sailing. They were able to increase the number of sails attached to the mast, which not only made ships easier to steer but also more powerful. They also made a significant change in the way that boats were constructed. The Egyptians had simply fitted together grooved planks of wood to form the ship. The Greeks improved on that plan by building

a skeleton for each vessel and then fitting the planks into the established frame. This advancement made for a more solid vessel with enhanced capability for handling rough waters. Several centuries later, the Roman ships dominated the seas. At 180 feet (55 meters), their ships were not as long, but they were more powerful, capable of carrying more than 1,000 tons (910 metric tons) of cargo.

The Roman ships that dominated the seas about two thousand years ago had sails attached, but, as the Greeks had done in previous centuries, the Romans got most of the power on their ships from oarsmen. On the largest ships, well over a thousand slaves and prisoners were used for rowing. This large-scale use of manpower added hundreds of tons of weight to the ship, decreasing its speed. The presence of such a crew also required a ship with a very wide hull, and that prevented it from maneuvering well through ocean waters.

In the thirteenth century, a major advancement took place when a rudder was added to the back of ships. This replaced the previous steering technique, which used oars on the side. In the fifteenth century, a significant development in design was made with the creation of the "full-rigged" ship. It had bigger square sails on the front and middle masts, with a lateen, or triangular sail, on the back mast. This type of ship was used by the famous explorers of the fifteenth and sixteenth centuries, including Christopher Columbus, Ferdinand Magellan, and Vasco da Gama.

As ships became more proficient at using the wind, the need for huge forces on board gradually diminished. By the end of the eighteenth century, the large

*OPPOSITE: **A full scale replica was built of one of Christopher Columbus' ships, the Santa Maria. Though its design is not nearly as sleek as later sailing ships, this type of vessel served most of the famous explorers of the fifteenth and sixteenth centuries.***

galley ship had disappeared completely. The sail-powered ships that replaced them were quicker and easier to control in all conditions, especially in rough seas. These factors made the sailing ship particularly more successful than the galley ship when engaged in combat. On commercial vessels, the largest sailing ships were so efficient that they did not require as large a crew. The biggest sailing ship of the nineteenth century, the Roanoke, needed a crew of only thirty-five.

ABOVE: **This is an illustration of a sixteenth century ship built by Henry VIII, The Great Harry. The large living quarters in the back of the boat, and the much bigger ones in the front, made speeds at sea quite slow.**
OPPOSITE: **In 1995, to commemorate the 375th anniversary of the original Pilgrims' landing in Massachusetts in 1620, this ship called the Mayflower II simulated the original Mayflower and sailed into Cape Cod Bay.**

Warships Under Sail

Throughout the history of sailing, most large vessels have been designed to be prepared for battle, even if they were not in military service. Pirates, marauders, and enemy warships posed enough threats at sea that all vessels had to be ready for possible assaults of all sorts. In later times, most large ships, even when not on military missions, always needed to carry weapons on board to fend off attacks.

In the earliest days of naval warfare, conflicts at sea were usually quite similar to battles on land. Instead of firing artillery at an enemy, sailors from one ship would cross over and engage the enemy's crew in hand-to-hand combat. Later the Greeks attached a hard, sharp point to the front of their ships and used it as a ramrod to disable an opposing ship. This ancient practice was still in effect and still working more than two thousand years later.

By the sixteenth century, the major navies of the world needed ships that could move quickly to avoid or seek out enemies. But they also had to be strong enough to house large armies, carry heavy artilleries, and withstand attacks. By the beginning of the seventeenth century the Dutch fleet was the most powerful on the seas. But in that century's conflicts, Dutch dominance at sea would fall to the British ships, which were sturdier and possessed more firepower.

OPPOSITE: **As shown here in this eighteenth century painting by John Pine, the Spanish Armada was defeated by the English in 1588 in one of the most famous battles ever fought at sea. The ramifications of this battle were felt for centuries, as the English became the supreme power on the world's oceans.**
LEFT: **This painting by an unknown French artist shows a flotilla of Dutch warships at sea, towering over smaller vessels.**

In subsequent centuries the major nations of Europe continued to develop ships in a desire for maritime superiority. Artillery aboard naval ships increased in size. By the seventeenth century, battleships were carrying armaments so heavy that they had to be designed differently from other large sailing ships. By the eighteenth century, Great Britain, which had the world's most effective navy, built warships that carried more than one hundred cannons, requiring much stronger decks for support than on nonmilitary ships. The British ships were considered of inferior design, especially in comparison to the French ships. But the British ships possessed artillery that was better designed and more efficient. They also improved their own ship designs by examining the foreign ships that they captured in combat.

In the eighteenth century the main weapon at sea was the cannonball, the largest of which weighed about 42 pounds (20 kilos). But it would take several shots of even the biggest cannon balls to break down a large ship. The more dangerous aspect of the attack was the scattering of debris, which often caused the ignition of a ship's gunpowder.

*They are ill discoverers that think there is
no land, when they can see nothing but sea.*

—FRANCIS BACON

ABOVE: **Battleships, such as the one seen here, had to be built with extra
fortification, both to withstand attack and to carry heavy armaments.**
OPPOSITE: **The French battleship, Bretagne, with its large crew and huge
armaments, is pictured here at the fort of Cherbourg. The overall
design of French warships was considered superior to that of the British.**

RIGHT: **The British artist W.T. Baldwin portrayed a number of England's most striking battleships in this nineteenth century work. Among the ships displayed are the H.M.S. Edgar, Liverpool, and Black Prince.**

Behold, now, another providence of God.
A ship comes into the harbor.

—WILLIAM BRADFORD

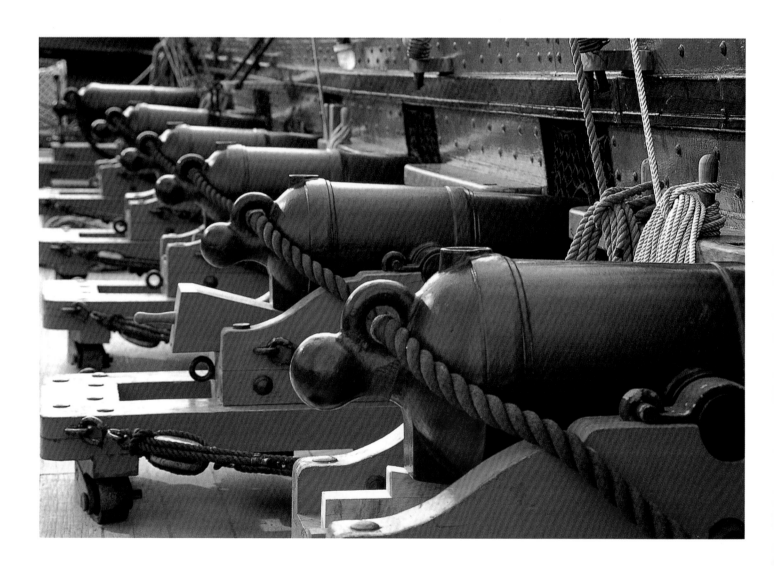

ABOVE: **The Constitution did not carry as much weaponry as larger battleships of its era, but it was very successful in combat, firing thirty-two pound cannonades from the cannons shown here.**
OPPOSITE: **The USS Constitution, which played such an important part in United States naval history, is shown here in its restored state.**

The centuries of warfare under sail concluded in the nineteenth century. Among the last great conflicts of tall sailing ships was the famous Battle of Trafalgar in 1805, won by British ships against the combined forces of Spain and France. The British ships may have been of inferior design, but that was overcome in part by the superior discipline of their sailors. The other big advantage of the British ships was the higher quality of their admirals, particularly Lord Nelson, who was killed near the end of the battle on board his ship, H.M.S. *Victory*.

The grand scale of the Battle of Trafalgar taught many lessons about the vulnerability of warships. In the following years, the navies of Europe made further improvements to their ships that increased their power while further fortifying them from attack. The last great battle of sailing ships was at Navarino Bay, Greece, in 1827, in which the superior British fleet defeated a Turkish navy.

By the middle of the nineteenth century the wooden-hulled sailing ships that had been used by the navies of the world for centuries were quickly phased out. In the quest for survival at sea, the sentimentality among commercial builders and designers for wooden-hulled ships was not an issue with warships. The creation of more deadly explosives meant the combustible wooden-hulled ships were too vulnerable, and they were quickly replaced by iron hulls. And once steam-powered ships proved superior in combat, they replaced all sailing warships.

In the modern navies of the world, sailing ships are still used for the training of new officers. Even though all their future work will be on other types of vessels, it is still believed that new officers trained under sail will receive a better understanding of how to control any ship at sea.

OPPOSITE: *The famous battle at Trafalgar in 1805 was won by the British forces, due to the superiority of their admirals, especially the British fleet commander, Lord Nelson, who was killed in the fighting. The battle in all its violence is depicted here by the British artist, Joseph Mallord William Turner.*
RIGHT: *The composure and strength of Admiral Lord Nelson are evident in this portrait of him with young Horatio Nelson. It was painted in 1799 by a British artist, Guy Head.*

*ABOVE: **Until weapons became much more accurate and deadly, the usual military attack attempted to ignite a fire on the opposing ship. Such an act is shown here in a work by Konstantinos Bolanchi, Loss of the Ajax off Cape Janissary.***

ABOVE: **The British artist John Thomas Serres made this portrait of a British man-of-war on the open sea. Though not the best constructed for battle, the superior command of the English admirals made them the most successful fighting ships for several centuries.**
OPPOSITE: **The fleets of the French and English, which fought in some of history's most famous naval conflicts, are shown here firing at each other's line of ships. Because of this method of engagement, all significant warships were designated ships-of-the-line.**

We have fed our sea for a thousand years
And she calls us, still unfed.
Though there's never a wave of all her waves
But marks our English dead.

—RUDYARD KIPLING

RIGHT: *Pictured here in this work by the Dutch artist Ludolf Bahuyzen is part of the Dutch fleet of the India company. These large, powerful ships could haul huge loads of cargo over great distances, though with very little speed.*
BELOW: *An East Indiaman ship, called the Thames, is shown at sea. The later clipper ships which took over the trade routes from the slower East Indiamen achieved greater speeds with higher sails and narrower hulls.*

Commercial Sailing

With Europe's discoveries and colonization of North America, South America, and Asia, the need increased for stronger ships to take advantage of the new avenues of commerce and carry home from distant ports such new products as silk, ivory, spices, and tea. The countries of Europe that took part in the new lucrative trade routes—most notably Portugal, the Netherlands, and England—used large ships known as East Indiamen. They were more than 150 feet (46 meters) long and, by the end of the eighteenth century, capable of carrying well over 1,000 tons (900 metric tons).

Before the nineteenth century, little emphasis was placed on the speed of large commercial vessels. Their owners' primary interest was to get their tremendous cargo home, so the ships were designed specifically for large, heavy loads, with no regard for graceful movement. The East Indiamen that traveled to the distant ports from Europe had an average speed of no more than 3 miles (5 kilometers) an hour. Trips to Asia and back often took more than a year. But eventually the British government, which had very protectionist policies, opened up its market to competition. After they did so, the builders of sleeker, quicker ships, known as China clippers or tea clippers, were able to take over

the distant trade routes. They made the trip back from the Chinese ports to Europe in under three months, about half the average travel time of the East Indiamen. And because they had not only the first supply of new tea but the freshest as well, customers were willing to pay more for their goods. So the ships delivering the product the quickest would get the most profit.

In the United States the demand for new clippers took off in the 1840s, spurred primarily by the discovery of gold in California. Early in that decade only one or two ships a year would make the trip from eastern ports to California. But with the discovery of gold in 1848, the demand grew dramatically. The level of gold

ABOVE: **The Cutty Sark, portrayed here on a voyage, had one of the most colorful histories of any ship. It traveled extensively to China and Australia during the nineteenth century, and continued in service well into the twentieth century.**

OPPOSITE: **Seen here on the bow of the famous restored clipper ship, the Cutty Sark, is the figurehead of a woman. Her appearance is based on the words of a Scottish poem for which the ship was named.**

fever was so high that it was often difficult to keep extra passengers off the departing ships. When ships reached port in San Francisco, the scene was even more out of control. Many passengers didn't wait to make an orderly disembarkation but just dived into the water to swim ashore to speed their arrival. Many members of the ship's crew had only taken work on board so they could get in on the riches themselves, and they also abandoned ship quite readily.

While the passengers were in hot pursuit of riches, the shipping and shipbuilding industries did not need to find any gold themselves to become huge beneficiaries of the gold rush. They made great profits from

ABOVE: **Etched here is the Earl of Balcarres, one of the many tall ships known as "East Indiamen," which took part in the lucrative Asian trade.**

OPPOSITE: **American artist Edward Moran captures a ship in motion, speeding forward with billowing sails, in his work, Passing Ambrose Lightship.**

passengers who were willing to pay exorbitant fees to get to San Francisco on the fastest ships. They also made big money from the greatly expanding community in San Francisco, which was desperately in need of supplies. Ships arriving in the area from eastern ports could sell enormous quantities of basic cargo at highly inflated prices. Products were sold for at least ten and sometimes up to a hundred times their normal selling price.

The demand for ships was so high, and the rewards for ship owners were so huge, that the shipbuilding industry in North America expanded greatly. With the profits to be made selling goods to the California settlements, the new ships not only had to have the speed of the China clippers that had been built a few years before, but they also had to be big enough to hold a large load of cargo. They also had to be sturdy enough to handle the treacherous conditions of Cape Horn at the bottom of South America. Hundreds of new clippers were built to handle this demand, and no matter what their cost, it could be made up quickly with just

RIGHT: *An early clipper, Virginian, is shown in this illustration. Later, the format of the three square sails seen here was improved by dividing the two highest sails.*

a voyage or two. After they unloaded their cargo in California, many clippers from the eastern ports would continue on across the Pacific, where they would pick up further profitable loads of cargo.

The golden era of tall ship construction did not last very long. In the 1850s, a railroad was completed through the isthmus of Panama. That made it possible to take a steamship to the eastern coast of Panama, take a train to the other coast, and then board another steamship to California. This new way of getting to the gold in San Francisco took only about five weeks, saving about two months over the best time of the clippers. Naturally it took over the great bulk of the passenger service. With the shrinking demand for their services, many of the clippers built in the frenzy were dismantled.

ABOVE: **The Yankee clippers constructed in the nineteenth century were the fastest wooden sailing ships ever built. A Yankee clipper is seen in this work of an unknown artist called, The Ship Nancy, Homeward Bound.**
OPPOSITE: **The distant route from Europe to the riches of the Chinese ports was sailed for centuries until the opening of the Suez Canal allowed steamships to take control of the trade. A clipper ship is shown in this work by Montague Dawson, Dawn and a West Wind in the China Seas.**

Dangers and Cruelty at Sea

The weather was always a major threat at sea. Before sophisticated forecasting, communications, and radar, the dangers of storms at sea were enormous. It was not unusual for ships and their crews to vanish without a trace. The normal procedure for a sailing ship in heavy weather was to take down its highest sails and use just one of its lower sails on each mast. This would allow the ship to continue on its course but would take pressure off the masts, which were already under severe stress from gale winds. These techniques were usually successful, but not always.

Among the most dangerous areas for sailing ships was Cape Horn, which had long stretches of heavy winds caused by a meeting of weather patterns from the Atlantic and the Pacific, with the mountainous terrain of Antarctica and South America beating the winds back and forth. The total number of ships lost in that region was never accurately counted. There were other treacherous areas, including the currents off the coasts of England. One of the worst disasters at sea occurred out of Liverpool in 1854, when the ship *The City of Glasgow* vanished with its total of 399 on board. Other waters not usually as dangerous could

become so quickly in bad weather. In 1867 a hurricane struck the West Indies in the Caribbean, sinking fifty-eight ships and killing about a thousand people.

Even if a sailor was able to survive the threats of nature, he would encounter plenty of man-made problems onboard ship. Civility, fairness, justice, and lawfulness were, until late in the nineteenth century, ideals rarely implemented on the seas. With total authority, many captains were very strict, provoking the occasional mutiny. But one of the reasons for the strictness of many captains was the nature of their crews. Until recent times, ship's crews did not include well-polished graduates of naval academies. Many of the crew members of the past were criminals pressed into service because of the need for any able body. Others were "impressed," that is, virtually captured on land and carried on board to work. Still others who went to sea were escaping whatever troubles or threats faced them at home. And there were those who joined crews of ships heading for gold rushes and other potential riches who did so only to get in on the wealth for themselves,

with little regard to how well they worked on the ship. With these types of crews, it becomes more understandable that many captains needed to enforce strict discipline to keep such groups in line, though that does not excuse the cruel excesses of some captains.

In 1879, after it had already been barred by most countries, flogging of sailors was banned on all British

ABOVE: **James Butterworth captures a dramatic moment in his depiction of a clipper ship caught in rough seas. Notice that the captain has taken down all but two of the ship's many sails, mostly to save them from damage.**
OPPOSITE: **Even the largest wooden ships were not able to overcome the heaviest storms. George Phillip Reinagle captured such a moment in this early nineteenth century work, First Rate Man-of-War Foundering in a Gale.**
FOLLOWING PAGE: **This painting by Edward Moran portrays the calm after a storm. The tranquillity of the sky belies the frantic nature of the repairs needed on board after damaging weather.**

That dolphin–torn, that gong–tormented sea.
—William Butler Yeats

ABOVE: *This James Butterworth work is entitled, Square Rigged Ships Off Jetty. Notice the highest sails were not set, a procedure followed when maximum speed was not needed, or when weather conditions were very heavy.*

OPPOSITE: **One of the most famous clipper ships of the nineteenth century was the Rainbow,** *which perished at sea, as seen in this work by Russian artist Ivan Aivazofsky.*

ships, ending a cruel practice used through the ages to mete out discipline. Whippings were frequently arbitrary, often given for the slightest offenses, and totally at the discretion of the captain. The whole crew was required to assemble to watch the punishment handed out, to take notice of what could happen to other crew members if they didn't carry out their orders.

Commercial ships at sea were also subject to the threat of attack from other ships. Stories of marauders and pirates at sea go back many centuries. In the distant past, navy ships would loot cargoes of ships from other countries. Later, renegade individuals broke away from their ships or their navies in search of easier money than they were getting from their poor-paying sea work. Among the more notorious pirates of the past were Captain Kidd and Bluebeard, two formally "respectable" Englishmen who turned to the easier if eventually less secure life of crime. Working late in the seventeenth century and early in the eighteenth century, both were eventually captured and executed.

By the nineteenth century, much of the pirate activity took place in the sea hub of the Caribbean. The many islands provided good refuge for them to lay in wait for unsuspecting cargo ships. Pirates not only

seized possessions in their sieges, but often killed the crew as well. Finally, in the 1820s, the work of navy fleets from the United States and England cleared the Caribbean of these criminals, usually disposing of them without a trial. The navies of other countries also dealt swift justice to any pirates who assaulted their ships. But though attacks were all but eliminated from the Caribbean, there were still other areas of lawlessness on the world's seas. The most notable problems were in the harbors of China and other Asian passages where many tall ships carrying large cargo were assaulted. There were hundreds of incidents a year until the ruling British government of Hong Kong ordered a crackdown in the 1850s.

Thus, by the end of the nineteenth century, much of the cruelty and lawlessness that had been such a large part of sailing history had disappeared. Countries and their navies finally had the will, the humanity, or, eventually, the financial motivation to stop it.

The Twilight Era

After the ascendancy of the steamship, sailing ships went in yet another direction at the end of the nineteenth century. The use of steel hulls made them bigger and much stronger. These new sailing ships were not as fast as the clipper ships of the preceding decades, but their capacity for carrying cargo was

ABOVE: **One of the busiest docks in France is shown in this eighteenth century work by French artist Claude Joseph Vernet, entitled, Port of Marseilles.**
OPPOSITE: **Intrusions on board ships by marauders were common until well into the nineteenth century. An unknown artist pictured a typical assault in this work entitled, Melee on Board the Chesapeake.**

much greater; they could haul 7,000 tons (about 6,400 metric tons) or even more. The strength of these sturdy ships was such that the normal bad weather and rough seas, which could cause serious problems for wooden-hulled sailing ships, were no longer a major concern.

The largest of all sailing ships was the steel-hulled *Preussen*, built in Germany in 1902. Stretching a remarkable 433 feet (132 meters), the *Preussen* was the only sailing ship with five functioning masts. It had a cargo-carrying capacity of 8,000 tons (about 7,250 metric tons). Even with its overwhelming size, the ship worked so efficiently that it required a crew of only forty-seven.

Despite the power, size, and dependability of the *Preussen* and the other large steel-hulled ships, the commercial market for such vessels dried up early in the twentieth century, particularly after the opening of the Panama Canal in 1914, which made trips around South America through Cape Horn unnecessary. The steel-hulled ships had handled such trips with unprecedented ease, and the new canal, with its patches of calm sea and air, was of no use to sailing ships. So the glorious era of sailing came to an end.

ABOVE: **This nineteenth century work, by British artist Andrew Nicholl, shows one of the world's busiest passages between the Mediterranean and northern Atlantic ports, the Straits of Gibraltar.**

OPPOSITE: **This work by an unknown artist depicts a vessel nearing land. Seamen on board looked constantly to the horizon for a coast line, while those on land waiting for the ship also had scouts scouring the sea for any sign of an incoming vessel.**

FUNDAMENTALS OF

TWO

THE GREAT SHIPS

Building a large wooden ship required a good deal of planning as well as a massive job assembling the parts. Many builders worked from designs, others from models, actually half-models, since one half of the ship would have to match the other. Ship models were built anywhere from one to ten percent the size of the proposed vessel. The models took more time to create than the drawings, and unlike drawings, there were a lot of problems for the builders if the models were not painstakingly accurate. But the three dimensions of the half-model had the advantage over drawings of showing the shape of the ship, especially the hull. And originally it was easier for the builder to work from a model rather than decipher the numerous lines and measurements of a thorough sketch. But by 1870, as ship design became more sophisticated, models were no longer used. Builders insisted on precisely drawn architectural lines.

Ship Construction

The first and most important step in ship construction was getting the proper timber for the ship. The wood selected had to mature enough to be of the proper strength. Some shipbuilders were not as careful with the wood they selected, using immature wood that did not hold up against the rigors of the sea. The best time to cut down trees for shipbuilding was in the winter,

OPPOSITE: **One of the world's outstanding tall ships is this Norwegian vessel, the Christian Radich. It is shown here moving gracefully through choppy seas.**

when the sap in the tree was concentrated in the base. The wood had to be dried completely in the sun and then properly treated to avoid rotting.

The most successful wood for shipbuilding was teak, which was as strong as any wood and quite able to withstand the effect of continuous contact with the sea. If teak was unavailable or too expensive, the next preferred wood was oak. Other parts of the ships used different woods than the hull. Maple and elm were usually used on the keel because of their superior buoyancy.

As forests were cleared for shipbuilding and many other uses, choices of wood became fewer. By the eighteenth century, wood in Europe became less available, which is why large-scale shipbuilding became a major enterprise of the British colonies of North America. With the abundance of wood then available in North America, as well as other natural supplies, the North American colonies became the lucrative source of supplies to the shipbuilding nations of Europe, both to their ruling country of England and to England's military enemies. Shipbuilders had to be careful which woods they used, however, since at first they weren't familiar with many of the new types of timber being cut down and not all the wood turned out to be of sufficient strength for ship design.

After the many pieces of wood to be used were cut to precise measurements, the heavy labor of constructing the ship began. The first step was placing the parts of the keel. The sides, or ribs, of the ship were then fitted onto the keel. Then the various decks of the ship were laid. Following that work, the rudder and wheel were attached, then the anchor and all other parts. After

such matters as sail strength, wave resistance, and ship stability were not completely effective because of the constantly changing conditions encountered at sea. But nineteenth-century designers did find some general patterns that proved effective in increasing sailing speed.

One of the major changes was made to the shape of the ship's hull. The idea of lengthening the hull to increase speed had been mentioned by designers for centuries, but it was the builders of clipper ships in the nineteenth century who put it into practice. Sharpening the front point was another change to the hull that increased speed. There were also alterations made to the balance of ships by changing the placement of the widest part of the ship, known as the beam, and then narrowing it. So the ratio of a ship's length to its width, which had been 4:1 before the giant clippers, went to 5:1 and even 6:1.

completion and before the ship was painted, the structure was secured by applications of tar, copper, and caulk, then further fastened with specially designed bolts. When the new construction was complete, the ship was pushed to a different wharf, where the rigs and sails were attached.

Designs for Speed

In their quest to get more speed out of their boats, shipbuilders made continuous design changes. Shipbuilding was not just a science but also a craft and an art. The mathematical formulas used to determine

A lean and long hull, coupled with sails strung very high, had previously been considered an impossible combination at sea. The old theory was that a narrow hull would not be sturdy enough to keep a ship with tall sails under control. But the largest clipper ships built in the nineteenth century—known as "extreme" clippers because of their length—proved that this design not only could work, but could produce a ship capable of sailing much faster than any other.

Other tweaking was done to the keel, or the bottom of the ship. A V-shaped bottom was thought to be necessary to get a ship through heavier water, but a flat bottom proved superior for speed. Other changes were made to the stem and the stern (the front and back), which allowed for better handling through rough seas. Experiments were also made altering how much of the

*ABOVE: **As sailing ships became larger, with bigger and higher sails, they were able to handle rougher waters with more effectiveness. The British artist Montague Dawson shows here a ship called the Racer, going through heavy seas in a work titled, Swinging Along.***

*RIGHT: **In the quest for speed in ships built in the nineteenth century, the hull was made leaner and the bow was made sharper. Both of these elements are still used today on modern sailing ships, as seen in this ship of Poland, Dar Mlodziezy.***

ship stayed under water. The closer the top of the hull was to the waterline, the faster the ship sailed. And when the ship's hull was designed to go deeper underwater, it gave a marked increase to the stability on board.

Carved Figureheads

The practice of adding figureheads and other designs to ships dates back to the beginnings of sailing. The ancient Egyptians and Greeks put figureheads of religious significance on the front point of their ships. Roman vessels carried bronze godheads on board. And the Vikings also adorned the front of their ships. A figurehead was viewed by those sailing on board much as soldiers on land would view a coat of arms. It represented a symbol of what they were fighting for, or under whose protection they were sailing. With the superstitions of the sea, figureheads

OPPOSITE: **The galleon ship, developed during the Renaissance, allowed for larger forces on board with more protection. This artifact from Toulon, France shows the elaborate construction and ornamentation of the French galleon.**
BELOW: **Figureheads such as this, placed on the bow of the ship, gave the impression that it was leading the ship through whatever rough seas might be encountered.**

often became a symbol of good fortune—or sometimes bad—for those on board.

By the time the great clipper ships were created in the middle of the nineteenth century, ship carving was a profitable though highly specialized craft. Carving was done not just for the front of the ship, but also to provide ornamentation to other parts of the vessel. But the figurehead attracted the most attention. To create a

figurehead, a designer usually worked with one tree trunk, generally pine because other woods would wear out too quickly. The base of the figure was constructed to allow it to be slipped under the bow of the ship. To be noticed against the large ship, figures were literally larger than life, usually 7 to 8 feet (2–2.5 meters) tall, and about 3 feet (1 meter) wide. The most extravagant figureheads could become worn very quickly while traveling through rough seas and heavy weather, so parts of their form were taken in at sea to avoid damage.

Normally, the carver would create a figurehead befitting the name of the ship. If the vessel was named for a person, his or her likeness might grace the prow. If named for a bird or an animal, the carving would resemble that creature. On military ships the figurehead often featured a national symbol. On most ships, female figures were very popular diversions for male crews, who were often away at sea for a year or more. The big English ship the *Cutty Sark*, named for the clothing of a temptress of legend, featured the form of such a woman on its figurehead and on other parts

of the ship. There were also lions, dragons, angels, and religious symbols, as well as more generic figures of sailors and lads.

By the end of the nineteenth century, as the tall wooden hulls were gradually replaced by steamships or steeled-hulled sailing ships, the opportunities for ship carving were disappearing. Soon the era of ship carvers was over, but the remnants of their works that have been preserved show the quality of their creations and the artistry they added to ships.

ABOVE: **In the golden era of tall ships, ornamentations made for ships often featured wildlife, particularly birds. Usually, like the eagle shown here, they were depicted in flight.**

OPPOSITE: **Among the features to be seen on the restored "Old Ironsides" are these elaborate carvings on its headboard.**

FOLLOWING PAGE: **Ornaments made for the bows of ships, such as this angelic figure, were usually eight feet or higher. Otherwise, they would not stand out enough to be evident on a large ship.**

ABOVE: **The Cutty Sark was in service more than fifty years, and now sits in permanent dry dock in Greenwich, England. The shimmering gold leaf used to paint the ship by its original owner, Jock Willis, again shines across the ship's hull.**

LEFT: **The remains of the USS Constitution, including the elaborate ornamentation of its bow, have been restored and preserved. It was nicknamed "Old Ironsides" for its success in fending off attacks during the War of 1812.**

Masts, Sails, and Rigging

The enormity of tall ships was quite evident in the size of their masts. They reached to heights well over 100 feet (30 meters), so the wood used to make them was segmented, usually into three parts. The joints connecting the segments had to be quite strong, since the consequences of weak mast poles could be catastrophic. Another sign of the mammoth size of these structures was the amount of rigging needed. On the tallest ships with the biggest sails, the length rigging wires could total more than 10 miles (17 kilometers). Learning how to handle all these wires was the most essential part of the training of all seamen. A complete knowledge of the intricacies of the rigging was necessary to set, trim, and fasten the sails and all their connected parts, including the braces and the yards. Any sails not firmly and securely set could lead to serious dangers at sea.

In the nineteenth century, important progress was made in the way sails were rigged. Advancements in the rigging wires allowed for better handling of sails. Rigging strings, which had been made of actual rope, were switched to wire, which made control of sails easier. There were two types of rigging used on tall ships: standing rigging, which consisted of wires that were not moved much as they held up the mostly stationary masts and yards, and running rigging, which was used to maneuver the sails and so received much more handling.

As masts and wires got stronger, the size of the sails could be increased, which made them more efficient. The pattern of sails was similar on all the masts on a tall ship. Up until the middle of the nineteenth century, there were four sails on a mast. The lowest sail was known as the foresail on the front mast, the mainsail on the middle mast, and the crossjack on the

LEFT: **The replica of the HMS Bounty is seen here without its sails, which allows for a better view of the elaborate and complicated system of wires and yards which must be properly utilized on all tall ships.**

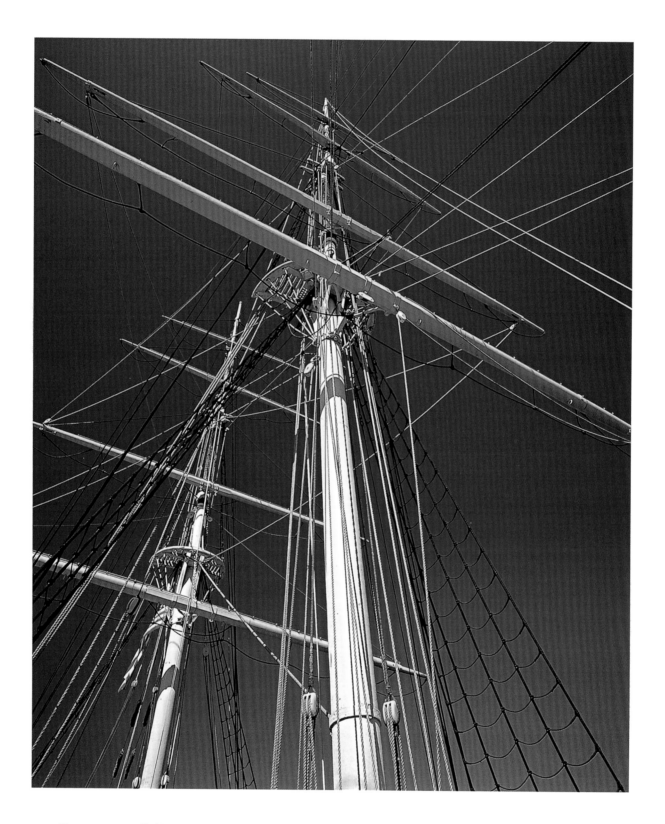

ABOVE: **The masts on tall ships are replete with numerous ropes, wires, pulleys, and strings.**

OPPOSITE: **The complicated nature of the rigging wires, as shown on this ship, required highly skilled "able" seamen to operate them properly.**

back, or mizzenmast. Above those sails were the topsail, the topgallant, and above them, the royal sail. Then in the 1840s, a British captain, R. B. Forbes, developed the idea of splitting both the topsail and the topgallant sails into halves, which made them easier to handle. As other advancments were made in rigging, these split sails were then increased in size, producing higher speeds on the water. Thus each mast then flew six sails, with each level of sail narrower then the one beneath it. Some of the largest ships flew even more sails above the royal sail, though that practice was discontinued late in the nineteenth century. In addition to the sails on the masts, there were also smaller, triangular sails, known as jibs, attached to the front of the ship, and a larger sail, known as a spanker sail, attached to the rear, or the stern. These additional sails gave added help to the square-rigged masts in utilizing the wind.

By the seventeenth century, the cloth used for sails was made of flax. It tended to be too weak and it also wore out quickly because it was not woven tight enough. Early in the nineteenth century, more sophisticated machinery enabled the production of stronger and more effective sails. It also became possible to make sails in higher quantities with consistent quality. The new, superior sails were made from a combination of flax and cotton. They were not only more durable, but also worked better than the sails made only of flax.

Even with these improvements in manufacturing, damage to sails was still a common problem, especially in heavy storms. As a result, a "sailmaker" (really a sail repairman) was an important part of a ship's crew. The sailmaker basically did the work of a seamstress, but with much more energy required. He had several specialized needles and a sharp knife for repairing tears. Some of his work with the largest sails required a good deal of strength, as well as needles powered by very strong handles or grips. As sails became more readily available and other sewing technology was developed, sailmakers gradually disappeared from the crews of almost all ships.

ABOVE: **The sails on tall ships, which tore easily before the nineteenth century, became stronger with the introduction of cotton into the fabric of the sail.**
OPPOSITE: **Without its sails, the ship Carthiginian sits quietly off the coast of Hawaii. This backlit forward view shows the vessel's complicated rigging in silhouette.**

OPPOSITE: **The famous American artist Winslow Homer captured a seafaring moment in this work depicting two men determining the ship's position with a sextant.**

BELOW: **In order to provide a feeling of authenticity on board the restored USS Constitution, a navy sailor poses, behind the ship's giant wheel, in the garb of a petty officer from the War of 1812, when the ship achieved its greatest naval successes.**

Controlling the Ship

Steering and navigation, the two activities that took up most of a captain's time, were both very difficult, painstaking tasks until recent modern equipment made them easier. An example of the type of rudimentary tools used by captains of the past was "the log," a way of measuring how fast a ship was moving. Centuries before the speedometer, a log was attached to a rope, thrown overboard for thirty seconds, and then reeled

back. The rope was measured, and calculations made to give a reading on the ship's speed.

It was important to know the exact location of the ship, known as the "dead reckoning." To help with that task, the sextant was developed, which helped to determine the longitude and latitude by measuring the ship's location in relation to the stars. It was also important to know the depth of the sea to help determine the ship's location. That information was especially useful in dense fog, when normal markings from the sun, moon, or stars were unavailable. A piece of lead weighing about 12 pounds (5.5 kilos) with a long line attached was tossed overboard. When the lead hit the bottom or the rope was stretched to its maximum, a reading was taken in fathoms, which equal 6 feet (about 2.8 meters). It was also helpful to know what materials were on the sea

floor, so the lead weight had a hollow portion containing a sticky substance that picked up seashells, mud, or whatever else was there. An experienced captain and first mate with a detailed knowledge of their route could read these findings and determine their location. Much more sophisticated tools have long since been invented, using an oscillator and a sound wave to determine ocean depths.

Before the advent of meters and gauges, steering a ship was a complex task whereby a captain's worth was truly measured. Since ocean winds are inconsistent, it was necessary to keep changing the path of the ship in order to obtain any speed. The ship had to be turned at a certain angle to the wind, a process known as "tacking." When making a sharp turn, the sails also had to be maneuvered quickly and constantly to allow the wind to help the ship, not work against it

RIGHT: **At sea with its sails fully unfurled, a tall ship required a skillful captain to change the directions of the sails in order to maximize the use of the wind.** *Japan's Kaiwo Maru is shown here.*

Working on Board

In control of all matters on board, the captain had to be a very experienced seamen to handle both his regular, awesome responsibilities and all the unexpected events that could happen at sea, especially on long voyages. When the captain gave commands, his main assistant, the first mate, was in charge of seeing that those orders were executed. The first mate was also in charge of designating both watch assignments and deck chores to the crew. Below the first mate was the thankless job of second mate. Not only did he hold down a full line of duties like the rest of the crew, but he was also responsible for carrying out the orders of the captain and first mate. Below the second mate were several others in charge of lesser assignments.

When at sea, there was never any shortage of work for a ship's crew. While the captain concentrated on steering and navigation and gave orders to carry out those vital tasks, other basic needs of the ship were handled continuously. The ship had to be kept as clean as possible, and any part of the ship might require repair at sea. Not only did sails and rigging have to be examined all the time, but cargo had to be checked constantly to make sure it was properly stored. Other crew assignments included a daily swabbing of the deck, which was done not just for appearance but to keep the wood of the ship from changing texture and weakening. It was also necessary to remove any sand that might have washed on board. All these and many other chores left the crew sore and weary by day's end.

It was more satisfying for a crew to tend to the sailing necessities of a ship. Among the many tasks were

ABOVE: **Today's sailing ships have all the modern conveniences which crews of previous centuries couldn't have envisioned. But much of the work with the wires and ropes is similar, as seen here as a crew works on the ship Gloria.**

OPPOSITE: **Skilled seamen move up the ladders of a tall ship docked in New York City. The weather here is fine, but such movements in stormy conditions at sea would be much more treacherous.**

FOLLOWING PAGE: **The men on the bow of this ship, who are dwarfed by the size of just a few sails, give some indication of the enormity of a tall ship.**

furling sails, handling rigging, and straightening and repairing ropes. Those in the crew most adept at such work were known, fittingly, as "able seamen." Their efficiency with the ropes and sails spared them of some of the drabber, more backbreaking work. In a typical crew of about fifty, there were usually only about six able seamen on board.

Surviving at Sea

Through the nineteenth century, the life of crew members aboard ships was not just difficult but downright dangerous. And the threats were not simply personal peril from dangerous heavy work or rough seas or from attacks by pirates and other enemies. There were also extreme problems of hygiene at sea. Diseases ran rampant, both from exposure to natural elements and from contaminated food and water. Typhoid, malaria, yellow fever, and scurvy were just some of the deadly diseases common on board sailing ships. This was an important factor in the great need for speed, because decent food was not abundant, and medical supplies, primitive as they may have been, would run out early in the ship's journey. The shorter the trip, the more likely the ship's crew could stay healthy, or at least survive the trip. There were instances of entire crews being lost to sickness while at sea.

In the days before refrigeration, meals aboard sailing ships were of the lowest possible quality. Even by the time ships had done a better job of dealing with contamination and nutritional needs, the facilities for the cook and the amount of food that had to be prepared for a fairly big crew hardly produced sumptuous meals. And in the cramped quarters of many ships, where all available space was used for cargo, meals were not exactly served to the crew in orderly dining halls. Seaman had their meals wherever they could find room.

Even in the unlikely event that the cook actually possessed some skill at preparing meals, he just didn't have enough good food to work with. The main staple of his preparations were huge slabs (almost more like boards)

of beef. In those prerefrigeration days the technique for preserving beef was to load it heavily with salt. Though it might have preseved it, this method did not prevent the meat from becoming rock hard, so it had to be soaked in water for at least a day before the cook could boil it. It was far from palatable, but those on board had no other meal options. In addition to the meat, each meal also included "hard tack," rock-hard biscuits that tested the strength of a sailor's teeth.

Not all the food was quite as bad as the meat and biscuits. The crew certainly appreciated any fish that had been caught or had washed on board, but there was rarely enough for all. Fruit and vegetables also made the meals more digestible, but usually they didn't last too many days on a distant voyage.

For all his efforts, the cook, like other specialized shipboard workers including the carpenter and the sail repairman, was given special treatment. Only in the greatest of sea emergencies would he take part in crew work. He was also sought out as a friend by many in the crew. Since he operated a stove for cooking, others on board hoped to be able to stand near its warmth during cold spells, or to help dry out after heavy storms.

Late in the nineteenth century, the tall ships found a better way of getting fresh food on board by bringing animals along. Chickens provided eggs, and cows provided milk. Goats were often brought on board as well, to provide milk and also to eat scraps and other remains requiring onboard disposal. Of course, certain animals were set aside for slaughter at sea to provide the crew with a reliable supply of fresh meat during a long voyage. The practice of bringing livestock on board ships to provide fresh food was still in place decades later on the first luxury liners.

OPPOSITE: **On the longest ships, the largest sails are very heavy and require the strength of several seamen to be moved and set. Here three crewmen struggle with a large canvas on the ship Gloria.**

ABOVE: **A modern day seamen is seen working on a ship's ropes. In the mid-nineteenth century, when so many clipper ships were being built, ship owners found it difficult to find enough able seamen for their voyages.**

OPPOSITE: **The dangerous task of operating a tall ship is evident in the huge number of seamen shown here working on a mast.**

LEFT: **The nineteenth century artist John Christian Schetky's rendering of a harbor shows the dramatic size of a tall ship compared to the yachts and merchant ships surrounding it.**

*ABOVE RIGHT: **The Kaliak-ra,** a ship of Bulgaria, seen at sea. This vessel is not technically a "tall" ship because it is square-rigged on only one mast.*

*RIGHT: **The Spanish ship,** Juan Sebastian De Elcano, features four masts, However, they are not all square-rigged, so they cannot maximize the power of the wind.*

*OPPOSITE: **The full crew of the ship Gloria poses** for this dramatic picture, as she passes in review*

We are as near to heaven by sea as by land!
—Sir Humphrey Gilbert

TALL SHIPS

LEFT: **Many of the tall ships are often gathered together for festivals in the world's great seaports. Newport, Rhode Island has been a frequent point for such gatherings, including the tall ship celebration of 1991, which included this large vessel.**
OPPOSITE: **This tall modern ship from Germany, the Gorch Fock, is seen here with its sails fully unfurled. The striking ornamentation on its bow features sea birds in flight.**

TALES OF THE

THREE

TALL SHIPS

In the last years of the eighteenth century, the navies of Europe used two types of large sailing ships. One kind was built to hold large armaments, thus decreasing speed and maneuverability. Another kind, known as a frigate, was built to hold less artillery but had greater speed. Frigates were used mostly for communications and intelligence work. They had just one gun deck, compared to the two or three on the biggest warships, and they also used lighter guns than the heavier ships.

Old Ironsides

When the very young United States made plans to construct warships in the 1790s, the decision was made to build six frigates. Their designer, Joshua Humphries, created them with more firepower than most other frigates. They were also designed to have the sailing capabilities of the best ships of the time. The most famous of the six frigates constructed at that time was the *Constitution*, built in a shipyard outside of Boston. When it was completed, it stretched for 204 feet (62 meters). The ship had nearly a 5:1 ratio of length to width, which accounted for its quickness: it reached speeds of nearly 15 miles (25 kilometers) an hour. Its largest sail, the mainmast, was more than 100 feet (30 meters) wide. The sails on all three high masts totaled more than 42,000 square feet (13,000 square meters) of flax.

LEFT: **The Constitution *is pictured here at full sail and in motion by the artist Joseph Clark.***

In its early years, the *Constitution* was used to ward off the pirates affecting American trade in both the Caribbean and the Mediterranean. When the War of 1812 commenced, the *Constitution* played an important part in the United States' naval success, engaging in combat with the British frigate the *Guerriere*. The *Constitution's* superior artillery was decisive in the conflict, as was the superior design. The British artillery fired at the *Constitution* caused little damage to the well-built wooden hull. Legend has it that after a British sailor saw the ineffectiveness of the British weapons against the *Constitution*, he yelled out, "Her sides must be made of iron!" thus giving rise to the ship's famous nickname, "Old Ironsides."

Later in 1812 the *Constitution* had another famous battle with another British frigate, the *Java*. After damaging exchanges of firepower, "Old Ironsides" showed her superior maneuverability by moving around the *Java* and getting in a better attacking position. After a merciless pounding of artillery, the *Java* "struck her colors" (surrendered), but not before sixty of her crew were killed.

OPPOSITE: **The Sea Witch *was one of the first great Yankee clipper ships. Built in 1846, the ship traveled from North America to China at speeds unheard of before.***
BELOW: **The Constitution *is shown in battle with the British ship* Guerriere *during the War of 1812. The superior design and construction of the Constitution gave it better mobility than its opposition and made it more capable of withstanding attack.***

So, with her superior construction, the *Constitution* was highly successful in battle because she could withstand attack, maneuver well, and carry heavier armaments than the English frigates she fought. Her success, along with those of the other tall ships built by Joshua Humphries in 1797 (including the United States and the President) played a major part in the defeat of the British by 1815.

Because of the *Constitution's* important role in American history, there was much interest in the ship after her sailing days were over. In 1925 a public subscription paid for her restoration in a Boston shipyard. After the work was done, she was sent for permanent display in Boston, Massachusetts.

Sea Witch

John Griffiths was a respected ship designer whose work on naval architecture was considered the first important American book on shipbuilding. In the early 1840s he announced his new theory for increasing a ship's speed. He would lengthen the hull, sharpen its bow, and move the beam (the widest part of the ship) forward. Other shipbuilders at the time claimed that Griffiths's radical ideas would not work, but his own ships, and the many other long clippers ships that would follow, proved his wisdom.

Griffiths' first put his theories into his design of the *Rainbow*, usually thought of as the first extreme clipper. Launched in 1845, the *Rainbow* was built to travel from

LEFT: **Sovereign of the Seas** **was one of the largest Yankee clippers built in the 1850s. Such ships were called "extreme" clippers because of their enormous length and height.**

ABOVE: *During the great era of clipper ship building in the nineteenth century, their majestic appearance in a harbor could attract large crowds.*

OPPOSITE: *Pictured here in this Currier And Ives piece is the clipper ship* Red Jacket, *shown making its way through the icy waters of Cape Horn on her voyage to Liverpool from Australia in 1854.*

New York to the ports of China, which had just been opened for trade. Over the next several years the ship set numerous speed records on her long trips to Asia.

In 1846 Griffiths had an even bigger success with his next China clipper, the *Sea Witch*. At 170 feet (52 meters) and 908 tons (817 metric tons) the new ship was quite large for her time, though the extreme clippers built a few years later were much bigger.

Though larger ships would follow, none would travel any faster than the *Sea Witch*. On her first voyage in 1846, she sailed from New York to Hong Kong in just seventy-nine days, then came home in just eighty-one days more. The appearance of the ship stunned those in New York when she returned so quickly from a trip that, just a few years earlier, had taken twice as long. As word spread of her impending arrival in New York, many wondered if the *Sea Witch* had found some shortcut previously unknown. But it wasn't the route that was remarkable, it was the speed of the ship. The *Sea Witch* made an even faster trip in 1848, traveling home to New York from Hong Kong in just seventy-four days.

The *Sea Witch* had several advantages other famous clippers never had. Some very favorable winds increased her speed on her record-breaking runs. She also had the advantage of an outstanding crew, selected personally by her captain, Robert Waterman. Such a crew was not possible a few years later, when many more clipper ships were sailing and the supply of able seamen was spread thin.

After her triumphant voyages to China, the *Sea Witch* was diverted to a different route. In response to the demands caused by the San Francisco gold rush, she began sailing to California. She set another record on that route, becoming the first ship to reach San Francisco from New York in under one hundred days.

After a few more years of success while sailing both to San Francisco and China, the fortunes of the *Sea Witch* suddenly went very bad. In 1855 while sailing to Rio, her captain, George Fraser, who had taken over the ship from Robert Waterman in 1850, was murdered by his first mate. Then in 1856 the *Sea Witch* was totally destroyed when she crashed into a reef off the coast of Cuba.

Stag Hound

No great commercial ship of the past was created without the enterprise of a patron. The tall ships whose memories are most lasting were not just the result of many, many months of labor. The stories of the great ships are also about the men who had both the money and the knowledge and fortitude to get them built.

One of the most important of all ships designers was Donald McKay. Born in Canada, he built some fairly big sailing ships, known as packets, in the early 1840s. Then in 1844 he was hired by a Massachusetts financier, Enoch Train, who gave him his own construction yard outside the East Boston harbor. In that location, McKay constructed some of the biggest and most famous sailing ships of all time.

McKay's first extreme clipper was the *Stag Hound*, which first sailed from Boston Harbor in December 1850. With a length of 215 feet (65 meters) and a weight of more than 1,500 tons (1,360 metric tons), she was the largest vessel on the seas at the time of launching. An excited crowd of ten thousand watched as she sailed into harbor, led by her dramatic figurehead of, appropriately, a running stag. The *Stag Hound* was so big and so narrow that many doubted she could sail safely. Among the doubters were her insurers, who charged extra premiums to cover the ship. But merchants had more faith in her than the underwriters did. All cargo space on the *Stag Hound* was sold quickly, guaranteeing the ship's owner a huge profit with just her first voyage.

The *Stag Hound* had no particularly fast times on any of her voyages, mostly because she rarely had favorable winds. She also encountered some heavy storms, including a typhoon in the Pacific in 1853,

RIGHT: **Donald McKay achieved enormous success with several extreme clippers built in New England in the 1840s and 1850s. The Stag Hound was one of his most famous ships and the largest clipper in the world when it first sailed in 1850.**

Following the success of the Stag Hound, the Flying Cloud was Donald McKay's next creation. It was even bigger and faster than its predecessor, and set speed records traveling between New York and the gold rush in San Francisco.

which she battled for five days. But she made her way across the seas safely through the 1850s, traveling annually to San Francisco and the Chinese ports of Hong Kong, Shanghai, and Foochow.

In 1869 the *Stag Hound* was sold to a firm in Boston and she made her first run across the Atlantic to

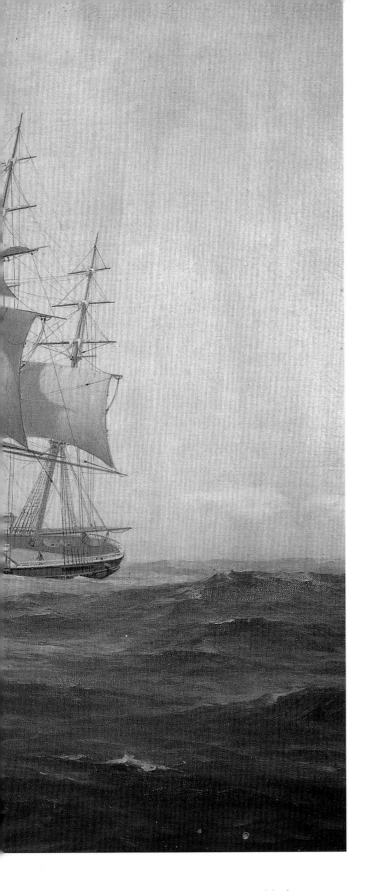

Flying Cloud

After Donald McKay's huge initial success with his first extreme clipper, he did even better with his next ship, the *Flying Cloud*. Another large crowd turned out for the launching in Boston in 1851. The new ship was even longer than the *Stag Hound*, by 20 feet (9 meters), and heavier, by almost 250 tons (225 metric tons). And not only was she faster than the *Stag Hound*, she would turn out to be faster than all other ships in the world.

Adorned with her figurehead of a white and gold angel, the *Flying Cloud* went down to New York after her launching to pick up a load of cargo for her initial voyage to San Francisco. The new clipper had many obstacles to overcome on that first trip. Most were caused by the difficulties of finding good crewmen in the 1850s. During that period, so many ships were sailing to the California gold rush that the supply of able seamen had been thinned out dramatically. There was also a good deal of bad weather on that initial voyage. Early on the ship sailed into a strong gale that tore off several of her sails. Later she encountered heavy snow in the south Atlantic. There was even a sabotage attempt on the initial voyage of the *Flying Cloud* that nearly sunk the ship.

The *Flying Cloud* had most of her troubles behind her when she reached the bottom of South America and made the turn north at Cape Horn. At that point her great speed became evident. In one day she covered 374 miles (570 kilometers), the longest run in a day by any kind of ship up to that time. And even with the earlier problems on the trip, the *Flying Cloud* made it to San Francisco from New York in eighty-nine days, a new record.

The next year the *Flying Cloud* set another speed record by sailing from San Francisco to Hawaii in less than nine days. In 1854 she broke her own record on the New York to San Francisco route by thirteen hours. She then sailed on to Hong Kong and set the speed record for that trip. *The Flying Cloud* continued in service for several more years until the outbreak of the American Civil War greatly disrupted commercial

London. Her owners hoped she would then get an assignment to Australia, but failing that, she was given a load of coal to carry to San Francisco. Unfortunately, well into the journey, the *Stag Hound's* coal caught fire from spontaneous combustion. The crew safely abandoned ship, but the *Stag Hound* was lost.

OPPOSITE: **With its enormous size, speed, and luxuries, the Great Republic was meant to be Donald McKay's masterpiece. But a fire before its first commercial voyage damaged the ship and repairs by the insurance company reduced its original size.**
BELOW: **The Flying Cloud is shown here at sea, where its huge sails utilized the wind better than any other ship of the time.**

sailing. She was sold to a ship owner in England, working the Australian trade route through the 1860s.

The *Flying Cloud* did not have the glorious conclusion that her accomplishments warranted. In the 1870s she was used to carry lumber. In 1874 while she was being repaired in a Canadian harbor, she caught fire and was all but destroyed. Whatever salvageable parts were left were sold for scrap.

Great Republic

After his great successes with the *Stag Hound* and the *Flying Cloud* as well as another clipper, *Westward Ho,* Donald McKay outdid himself with his next ship, the *Great Republic.* Much larger than his other clippers, the *Great Republic* was more than 100 feet (30 meters) longer than the *Flying Cloud,* and at more than 4500 tons (3900 metric tons), she was almost twice as heavy. Her cargo-carrying capability was 6000 tons (5400 metric tons), far greater than any other commercial ship yet built.

The launching of the *Great Republic* was such an occasion that it was declared a holiday in the state of Massachusetts. Schools were closed and children were brought out to the waterfront to watch the great event. Crowds arrived by boat, train, and all other methods of transportation then available. When the *Great Republic* appeared on the harbor,

it was greeted with the cheers of the crowd as well as saluting cannons.

Everything about the *Great Republic* was huge and grand. Her construction required more than 2000 tons (1800 metric tons) of oak, 1,500,000 feet (460,000 meters) of pine, and more than 300 tons (270 metric tons) of iron. Her widest sails were 131 feet (40 meters). At the time of her launching, she was not only bigger than all other commercial ships, she was also twice the size of any ship in the United States Navy.

The passenger accommodations on the *Great Republic* were also of the highest quality. The tables were made of marble, the furniture was covered with velvet, and the rooms, adorned with artwork, were lit through stained glass. With her size and elegance, the *Great Republic* was meant to be the greatest ship ever sent to sea.

The ship's first voyage was to be across the Atlantic to Liverpool. She had been towed to New York to receive her cargo for this initial trip. But just a couple of days before her departure, a fire broke out on a nearby wharf and spread quickly. Many ships in the area were burned, and eventually the *Great Republic*

also caught fire. Before the flames were extinguished, little remained of the ship above her waterline.

After the disaster the ship was turned over to her insurers, who then needed all of 1854 to have her rebuilt. But in the process her dimensions were shrunk considerably. The weight of the ship was lessened by more than 1000 tons (900 metric tons), and her cargo-carrying capability was decreased by more than 2000 tons (1800 metric tons). Even her figurehead of a mighty eagle was replaced with a simpler design.

After being rebuilt the *Great Republic* was sold to British interests. She then made her belated first voyage to Liverpool. In Europe her owners had a hard time finding locations to dock the ship because of her size, even reduced as it was. Later, during the Crimean War, she was used for transporting soldiers. Then in 1856 she had a successful run from New York to San Francisco, making better time than any other clipper on that route that year. Just how fast and how profitable she would have been in her original form could only be the subject of speculation.

The *Great Republic* remained active through the 1860s. She carried lumber and guano, and transported more troops, this time during the American Civil War. In 1872 she was heading to South America to pick up a load of lumber when she was damaged during a serious storm in the Atlantic. When she started to leak, her crew abandoned her somewhere near Bermuda. Thus ended the sailing days of a ship whose enormous potential was never realized.

As for Donald McKay, he continued building ships until 1880, but never again attempted anything on the scale of the *Great Republic.*

Roanoke

When the speed of the clippers was no longer a great asset because of the shorter routes of steamers, designers started building ships in a manner more like they used to, that is, with less speed and more power. The narrow hulls of the clippers limited their cargo-carrying capacity, so the new commercial sailing ships from the last years of the nineteenth century were wider as well as longer. They were able to carry much heavier loads, and though they did not have the quickness of the extreme clippers, they still reached decent speeds and handled heavy weather very well. The ones built in the United States were known as Downeasters. They were constructed mostly in the most northern New England state of Maine, where shipbuilding traditions were still hanging on. By that time most ships being built were either steamships or sailing ships made with steel hulls. But the builders of Downeasters were not only still using sail power but were also making their ships of wood.

The biggest of the Downeasters was the *Roanoke,* which was launched in 1892. All the dimensions of the *Roanoke* were enormous. At 350 feet (100 meters) long she was more than 100 feet (30 meters) longer than most of the clipper ships from earlier in the century, and required enormous quantities of pine and oak for her construction. Her ability to carry cargo was also much greater: she could haul 5400 tons (6000 metric tons), five to six times the capacity of most commercial clippers. Her size also required extremely big sails. Her biggest sail, the mainsail, was almost 100 feet

(30 meters) wide and could weigh as much as a ton when soaked by a storm.

Since she was built more for power than for speed, the *Roanoke* did not fly her sails quite as high as earlier clipper ships. But because her sails did not require as much attention, the *Roanoke,* like other Downeasters, did not need as big a crew. That meant that she could operate more economically and more profitably.

Generally, by late in the nineteenth century, sailing ships no longer carried goods like tea because they did not sell as well after losing their freshness on long journeys. Instead they carried larger, bulkier items such as wheat and rice, which were not time sensitive. Some tall ships carried much less agreeable cargo. One such item was coal, which was a mess to handle and often resulted in dark coal dust getting all over just about everything. Even more disagreeable was the cargo for the manure trade from the islands off Peru in South America. Once the guano was brought back by the clippers, it was sold as fertilizer. Needless to say, the odorous cargo made the task quite unpleasant for the ship's crew.

The *Roanoke* did not take part in the guano trade, since she sailed successfully on the long trips from her eastern American home to California, Asia, and Australia. After being first launched in 1892, she averaged about a trip a year until 1905 when she met her demise. The greatest risk to wooden ships was fire; the possibilities of a lantern or another flame being overturned or being ignited by a flammable substance were often realized with catastrophic results. With their thinner hulls, the mid-nineteenth-century clippers were at the greatest risk of combustion. But even the very sturdy *Roanoke* met her final fate in a fire in 1905, burning to pieces when at anchor in Australia. By that time almost no wooden-hulled clippers were still being built; steel-hulled ships, which were easier to construct and control, had taken over what was left of the commercial sailing market. And with the demise of the *Roanoke,* the era of the large wooden sailing ships was virtually at an end.

*Land was created to provide a place
for steamers to visit*

—BROOKS ATKINSON

ABOVE: **This painting by Xanthus Smith of two tall ships has in its background the ominous presence of a steamship which, with its superior speed and dependability, would take away most of the sailing ships' business.**

Cutty Sark

With the opening of the Suez Canal in 1869, the great era of the tall sailing ship in Europe was coming to an end. The European clipper ships that had sailed around Africa and Asia on their way to China could not travel as fast as the steamers cutting through the narrow opening of the new canal, which saved about

ABOVE: **The Cutty Sark, the famous China tea clipper of England, is shown on one of its numerous ocean voyages. Commissioned in 1869, she was still sailing in the early twentieth century.**

4000 miles (7000 kilometers) on the trip to the major Chinese ports. And because the steamships could return from China so much more quickly with the freshest crop, they could sell their tea for much better prices than the tea arriving much later by sailing ship. The best ship captains and builders also began to switch over to steamers because that was where more of the business was, and with it, the better-paying jobs. So, much as the original clippers of the 1840s had profited because they were so much faster than the heavy, lumbering cargo ships that preceded them, so, too, did the tall sailing ships lose their hold on the market to a faster service.

Though large sailing ships no longer controlled the market the way they had and were not as profitable to operate, there were still entrepreneurs in Great Britain in the 1860s willing to build them. Many of them had grown up with an appreciation of the splendid and noble nature of the large ships and still considered them very desirable possessions. A high level of competition existed among the British owners at that time to build and own the fastest ship. One of these British shipbuilders was Jock Willis, who in 1869 commissioned a ship he named after a Scottish legend, the *Cutty Sark*. Willis's main goal was to build a clipper that could sail to China faster than any other, particularly a clipper called the *Thermopylae*. That ship, which had been completed the year before by a building rival of Willis, George Thompson, was the fastest English clipper of the time.

When construction of the *Cutty Sark* was completed, it measured 212 feet, 5 inches (64 meters). The extra 5 inches (13 cm) was quite purposefully included because it made the *Cutty Sark* that much longer than the *Thermopylae*. Willis's ship weighed 963 tons (860 metric tons) and could carry 650 tons (570 metric tons) of cargo. Her highest sail reached about 150 feet (44 meters) in the air. Willis spared no expense in his desire to build the sturdiest and most lavish of all sailing ships. He insisted on using the best wood, the finest and most durable metal, and the highest-quality paint.

To Willis's disappointment, when his new ship was launched on her journey to China, she was not as fast as the *Thermopylae*. On the trip home from China, the Cutty Sark took 110 days, while the *Thermopylae* made the return five days quicker. More disappointing was the price for which the ship's cargo sold when it returned home. The steamships that beat the *Cutty Sark* home got much better prices with their fresher tea, and the *Cutty Sark's* load also did not sell nearly as well as the cargo from clipper ships of earlier eras. Nevertheless, the ship continued its journeys, and continued to try to pick up speed on the *Thermopylae*. After many tries, she was never able to beat her rival to China.

When the Chinese tea trade was taken over completely by steamships in the 1880s, the *Cutty Sark* finally gave up on that route. For the next several years the ship visited ports around the world, searching for any cargo she could find. To the lovers of sail connected with the ship, it must have been difficult to accept that one of the *Cutty Sark's* jobs was hauling coal to distant ports for use by military steamships. Then, after going through several different captains of varying abilities, and nearly being destroyed by a series of sea disasters, the *Cutty Sark* began making the route to Australia to transport wool. This became almost the last vestige for the commercial sailing ship, since, even with the Suez Canal, Australia remained too long a trip from Europe for the steamships.

In the 1880s, more than fifteen years after first competing with the *Thermopylae* on the Chinese trade route, the *Cutty Sark* was again in competition with that other English ship in the Australia wool trade. Finally, after years of frustration, the *Cutty Sark* proved her superiority, besting the time of the *Thermopylae* on the return trip from Sydney to London. The commercial trip from Europe to Australia went all the way around the globe since outbound ships went under Africa to reach Australia, but, because of wind patterns, returned by crossing the Pacific, going under South America, and then north in the Atlantic until reaching Europe. The *Cutty Sark* made the entire trip in 151 days of sailing. The return trip east took only 73 days, a full week quicker than the *Thermopylae*. And for the following decade on the same route, the *Cutty Sark* was always faster than her main rival.

The *Cutty Sark* was so durable that, remarkably, it was still sailing more than fifty years after it was originally launched. After twenty-six years under the ownership of Jock Willis, the ship was sold to a Portuguese

ABOVE: **A tall freighter moves through the ocean. Its square-rigged sails can be flown higher than triangular sails and produce greater speed.**

OPPOSITE: **Some of the effects of high winds at sea are evident in this picture. Once the bad weather subsides and the flood water is drained, the deck must be swabbed so that the salt from the sea does not weaken the structure of the wood.**

BELOW: **The American whaler, a smaller and sturdier ship, worked off the coast of New England in the nineteenth century.**

owner, who kept her in service as a merchant ship for another twenty-six years. Then, in a bit of disrepair, she was bought by a British captain, Wilfred Dowman, who lovingly restored her and turned her into a training ship for young British sailors.

Most of the wooden ships that weren't destroyed at sea were, like worn-out modern automobiles, stripped down for their parts when no longer of use. Others, like the *Cutty Sark's* great rival, the *Thermopylae*, were given the honor of an actual burial at sea. Renamed the *Pedro Nunes* by her last owner, the Portuguese navy, the *Thermopylae* was intentionally sunk in the Atlantic in 1907 after thirty-nine years of sailing. The *Cutty Sark* was given an even better tribute in retirement. It was placed in a permanent dry dock in Greenwich, England, in 1954. Her sails no longer fly, but her masts still rise toward the sky, and her gold-leaf paint, which was returned to her hull in restoration, shimmers brightly. Like an apparition, the *Cutty Sark* is the only clipper ship from the golden era that has survived intact. It is the lone relic from the era when tall ships sailed to all parts of the world, and, at their zenith, numbered in the hundreds.

TALL SHIPS TODAY:

Though the golden age of tall ships is now long past—their majestic silhouettes superseded by such modern behemoths as super tankers and giant container vessels—there still exist a few ships to remind us of the glory days of sailing. Most of these vessels are used by the navies of various nations as training ships for young sailors. It is felt that the skills of seamanship, as well as the discipline and cooperation needed for survival at sea, can best be learned by manning a tall ship.

A few other great sailing ships, such as the *Cutty Sark, Constitution, Star of India,* and *Victory* are permanently docked and serve as museums, attracting thousands of visitors each year.

No matter where they are found, the tall ships of the past and present continue to inspire us. A sampling of some of today's tall ships can be seen in the following pages.

RIGHT: **The Star of India, seen here in her home base of San Diego, California, is the oldest merchant ship still afloat. Dating from 1863, the Star of India narrowly escaped destruction more than once. She was preserved and restored in San Diego.**

FOUR

A PORTFOLIO

*Never a ship sails out of the bay
But carries my heart as a stowaway.*

—Roselle Mercier Montgomery

ABOVE: **A close look at the Amerigo Vespucci** *without its sails.* **This mammoth Italian**
ship is 330 feet (100 meters) long, and her rig reaches heights of 160 feet (50 meters).
OPPOSITE: **The Amerigo Vespucci,** *one of the largest sailing ships in the world today, is*
shown here in full sail, sporting the flag of its home country, Italy. **This steel-hulled**
ship was built in 1930 and is used primarily for naval training.

ABOVE: **The Kruzenstern of Russia is the largest of all modern sailing ships. Stretching 378 feet (117 meters), her mainmast at 162 feet (50 meters) is as high as a fifteen story building. The ship was built in 1926 and taken over by the Soviet Union after World War II.**

OPPOSITE: **Seen here is one of the world's newest tall ships, Mexico's Cuahtemoc, which was built in Spain in 1982. Used for training by the Mexican navy, the Cuahtemoc is 296 feet (90 meters) long, and her rig reaches 140 feet (43 meters).**

LEFT: **The Simon Bolivar of Venezuela is seen here gliding through ocean waters. The young ship, launched in 1981, measures 270 feet (83 meters) and carries nearly two hundred men of the Venezuelan navy.**

Sail, sail thy best, ship of Democracy.
Of value is thy freight, 'tis not the present only,
The Past is also stored in thee.
—WALT WHITMAN

ABOVE: **Norway's striking Christian Radich, built in 1937, is one of the fastest of all modern sailing ships. This popular ship has attracted large crowds in public appearances and was also seen prominently in the 1958 film, Windjammer.**
OPPOSITE: **A gathering of tall ships in Newport, Rhode Island in 1989 featured this old French vessel, the Belen. Built in 1896, the 180 foot (55 meters) ship has a very colorful history, having been owned by the Duke of Westminster and the Irish brewing magnate, A.E. Guinness. After more than eighty years in service, the Belen was preserved and restored in France.**

ABOVE: **Anchored in Boston is Sagres II, a ship built for the German navy in 1938 but seized by the United States after World War II. Later, she was bought by Portugal in 1962, which still operates her for training.**
OPPOSITE: **With a capacity for nearly three hundred on board, the Gorch Fock is one of the world's largest naval training vessels. Built in Germany in 1958, the Gorch Fock is 295 feet (90 meters) long, with a rig reaching 140 feet (43 meters) high.**

To see! To see! This is the craving of the sailor... I have heard a reserved silent man, with no nerves to speak of, after three days of hard running in thick water, burst out passionately, "I wish to God we could get sight of something!"

—JOSEPH CONRAD

LEFT: **The United States ship Eagle, seen here, is used for sail training by the American Coast Guard. Originally built for the German navy in 1936, it was appropriated by the United States Navy after World War II.**

ABOVE: **The Tovarisch *was originally part of the German navy. It was sunk in combat in 1945, but salvaged a few years later by the Soviet navy, which turned her into a training ship.***

OPPOSITE: **The Elissa, *constructed in 1877, is now a tourist attraction in Galveston, Texas. Among her many uses was hauling cotton out of Galveston in the 1880s. The Galveston Historical Society bought the ship in 1975, brought her to Texas, and restored her.***

FOLLOWING PAGE: **The Argentine ship Libertad *is not only one of the largest of all modern training ships, but also one of the fastest. Launched in 1959, the Libertad is an awesome 336 feet (103 meters) long, with a rig of 165 feet (51 meters).***

ABOVE: **Like most all modern sailing ships, the Gloria has a steel hull, a diesel engine and is used for naval training. Now part of the Colombian navy, the Gloria was built in Spain in 1968.** OPPOSITE: **The overwhelming physical presence of the Juan Sebastian De Elcano of Spain is captured in this photograph. The ship stretches a majestic 352 feet (110 meters), and her highest sail reaches 164 feet (50 meters) into the sky.**

*I remember the waves and the slips
    And the sea–tides tossing free
And Spanish sailors with bearded lips,
And the beauty and mystery of ships
    And the magic of the sea.*

—HENRY WADSWORTH LONGFELLOW

ABOVE: **The Esmeralda, at 353 feet (108 meters), is the second largest sailing ship in the world today. Built in Spain in 1952, the Esmeralda is the naval training vessel of Chile.**
LEFT: **A collection of tall ships is seen here as they gathered at a Boston pier in 1992.**

I must down to the seas again, to
   the lonely sea and the sky,
And all I ask is a tall ship and a star
   to steer her by,
And the wheel's kick and the wind's
   song and the white sail's shaking,
And a grey mist on the sea's face and
   a grey dawn breaking.

—JOHN MASEFIELD

RIGHT: **Photographed at sea is the Nippon Maru.**
This Japanese training ship which stretches 318 feet
(98 meters), dates from 1930 and was renovated in 1975.

INDEX